S
___

Edit

CW00868963

ISBN: 978-1-913642-73-0

The authors have asserted their right to be identified as the authors of this Work in accordance with the Copyright, Designs and Patents Act 1988

Cover design by Aaron Kent

Edited & typeset by Aaron Kent

Broken Sleep Books (2021)

Broken Sleep Books Ltd
Rhydwen,
Talgarreg,
SA44 4HB
Wales

Contents

Snackbox

Edited by:
Aaron Kent

Introduction

I started Legitimate Snack during the first lockdown of 2020. Essentially, I was looking for a way to be physically creative in publishing - which is not to say the typesetting, desing, and layout aspects of Broken Sleep aren't creative, I just wanted to explore a handmade alternative. That, and I'd always had a fondness for books that state the mechanisms of the book itself: fonts used, paper, paper weight, etc.

The name came from an episode of *The Good Place* where Eleanor sobs 'I'm a legit snack'. It stuck with me, having heard it a year before starting the imprint, and I almost felt like I had to make *something* just to use that name.

The first Snack, *SHITSHOW*, was my own poetry, because if I messed it up I'd only be messing up my own work, I wasn't testing the waters with somebody else's endeavours.

I was working and living in a school as a housemaster and English teacher at the time, which meant all the printing was free. This, as I'm sure you'll agree was a great opportunity to start the imprint. I couldn't imagine the love it'd recive in return.

I'm proud of every Snack here. And I'm indebted to every author.

Aaron Kent

LS001:
SHITSHOW

Aaron Kent

Legitimate Snack 001

Title: SHITSHOW
Author: Aaron Kent
Originally printed on:
Paper: Diamond White Fine Linen (135gsm)
Cover: Scarlet Cumbria card (270gsm)
Endpapers: Banana Thai tissue (40gsm)
Titles: Franklin Gothic Heavy
Text: Calibri

3 runs of 50

Psykos*/*((Girlyas))

I'm alone on the western front,
again,

I'm handcuffed to the shore
and I launch myself into
work. It won't

be long, gunslinger, won't be
years before the minotaur chorus
[we're the chorus, the slender
minotaur]

wounds.   You w/o me & us converging
                                 let us speak, let us, let us, let
                                 us

          speak plot.

Peninsula, you're cap smoke to the
right temple, it's early

easy morning. Operator, we only
phone the wrong numbers. My
daughter speaks in keys

now and she ain't & she is. And
you ain't. You certainly ain't.

Bone Idol

I've never set foot in a pub without boxing gloves and a can of socialism — they wanna split us by those who down pints and those that quaff — the working class is a rainbow is a taught violence — I've never set foot in a pub without a reason to vote — a terraced house tory is still a tory — a terraced house terrorist is a consequence of an iron fist — it takes a parliament to kill a dream and the daily mail to kill a kid — I've never crossed a picket line I didn't love — environmentalism is for the rich I sustain myself on pesticides — we've got slide tackles in our veins and yellow carded kids — thatcher killed my granddad we dream of feeding her asbestos — we've got community and a fried breakfast — put the kettle on — round 2 and no longer sparring — I've never loved a tory and I don't plan on going home

Aaron Dean

Look, the first step is to take the pension, shimmy it
Under your waistcoat while the vultures circle the
Watercooler; they ain't interested in your petty

Theft, o snow-driven vulture. The key is in the star
Signs, sheriff, in the way you present yourself.
The brave boys in blue bellowing obscenities out

The window watching whistling waves of threats
And a handgun shaking. You can hold a protest
In your own house if you got markers and a spitRoast piggie

polyps – they ain't the hurting kind,
The real stomp your skull like a grapefruit freshly
Soured good morning world today is a lovely day to

Notice how your hand trembles, how your knees
Shiver in Spring, how the sirens scream 'BEAT RAW
BEAT RAW BEAT RAW.' You're always one

Cheque short of a full bank statement short of a
Story shared while pilfering the evidence lockers
Of angel dust, ket, the strong stuff that keeps a perp

Cigarette burnt the time it takes to grow and heal
A tumour, a festering wound. Take the pension, hit
Them where it hurts, then spend the cash on a

Decent pair of gloves, a balaclava, and a silencer.
Cops love fingerprints, they collect them and
Store our differences. Keep yours to yourself.

Herlin-Bamlet

Light water graphite
sarcophagus; pacification
      of red, burns intra
-damp, it is late enough for dusk
      to stain you again,
      you are too young
to shed thyroid – we hoard bananas
forecast corrosion / body heat mummifies
summer, stings fulcrum pivot fulcrum.
      I'm twice melatonin;
circadin-bred pensionable sleep
abstinence / swaddle in rock
      armour – dressed
Blayais (
success is not knowing the names
of four bad crows). Curriculum skills
by the light of the silvery moon, a
physicist; I love you calling them 'the
dips' – 'bluebell woods', I 'the resevoir'
      left gleaming backpack
Thursday / legacy box. Approaching,
      I will outlive myself,
      you pipsqueak.

Snow Smear

You and I -- spread -- wafer thin
across hollow prism needles,
I love you with low visibility;
a pack of thermal gloves and

glow sticks. The banks are lit up
like bioluminescence at a wedding
or that baby bump glow
before the life change, here we

melt in time; torn I quit bleeding
so springtails may replace my
nervous system with an itch
so splendid it causes

us to tear off my skin
and cook it on the campfire. You
see, this is love: us eating my
flesh under platelet dark clouds

Contingency Plan: Red Circles (Ophelia)

Ivory sinks the plum's flesh into the gate
of heaven, weakness is present in every
    inch of the cheek. She has a foxes cry
            and crime to frost in the parlour, we
never call it the parlour, but I do ask parlez-vouz
    Francais? Her tongue is undone by a run
of weak spots and sun spots in antithesis of
            dialogue, and it's no wonder
she truly speaks fox. The weight of heirlooms
    we can never offer because we can
never offer, because we can never stop
            collecting junk in the hope it means
        something. I am holding her first tooth
and you are present with anaesthetic.

Small, Wingless

I was born on a two piece
pay later, an interest
rate dictated by my
birth centile. I was breeched
in instalments, spread
across the year; my mother

birthed an overdraft limit,
christened the mass in
common tongue. Learnt
to make space a premium,
notched into the damp
like a silverfish pedalling

into the core of us. My
mother's loss in the plaster-
board shaped like every
pet we begged to need
us. My father counting
grief in a shell in the roof,

      the difference between
      me and a mortgage
      is that gutting a house
      takes time.

Levant 1919

Other materials, even in iron
pressed fatigue. The calm
precedes the storm precedes sleep
stretched so thin it is broken
in twilight. Home is void by work,
miners are void by pattern.

Full of intent, patterns
of populace against iron
for the sake of cheap work.
Cracks spread across calm
chatter, the bulk of broken
beams turn'd loose in sleep,

so deep to be eternal sleep.
Every timber leaves a pattern
neither confirmed nor broken
in the wake of the iron.
There is a permanent calm
with the permanent loss of work.

Choked by the need for work
in the palm of dead; sleep
as insurance against calm
infinity. the depth of patterns
in the onyx of an iron
wall. The rods are made to be broken

and rebuilt to be broken
again. Across the soiled work
tundra, run beneath iron
rain scalding the dreams; sleep
tonight in delicate pupils. Pattern
patchwork fields for the rest, calm

to be laid upon the sweet, calm
soil. Tin prices are made to be broken
and lost as prayers spread pattern
across a duchy sky. The end of work
and the frightful, long sleep
of an anxious walk to ruin. Iron

every calm friend lost to work
into all of the night's broken sleep.
Press their pattern deep with iron.

LS002:
Glib & Oil

Dominic Leonard

Legitimate Snack 002

Title: Glib & Oil
Author: Dominic Leonard
Originally printed on:
Paper: Woodstock Betulla (110gsm)
Cover: Carruba Nettuno Linen (280gsm)
Endpapers: White Translucent Vellum (100gsm)
Titles: Caviar Dreams
Text: Blacker Text

1 **run of** 40

Death Poem

I dreamed I was on a pier with Ingmar Bergman,
We must have been in one of his early films
As everything was black and white.

He was irritable because I was
Bothering him with questions and he was doing something
With rope and tools.

What are your films about?
I asked. He sighed
And put the tools down. TIME, he said,

And pay attention to the water.
But I don't remember any water in Wild Strawberries (1957), I said,
And only the beach scene in The Seventh Seal (1957).

Then you weren't watching closely, he said, and besides,
I've more films than that. He went back to his work.
Later, as he tied those great black knots, he said:

Watch the way the water behaves. You'll see
What they are about; seeing each other,
How you see through things, reflection. Ah!

I said, so they are about more
Than just TIME! Well, he said, looking out at the sea,
Perhaps you have got me there.

Dramatis Personae

Chorus of those who have seen the light played by those
        who have not
Oracle, or similarly oracular being
Lovers
Thin and open sheaves of light, sparsely so
Inconsolata (various)
Prayers, licked with hot applause
Those who have not
Dancers
Raincloud
Raincloud my hymnal

Ape of Form

So long
the hour adheres to my purpose:

to have known suffering
nebulously, kept our life bound

by the mutations
of dominion and great buildings

ossified, pedestals
illustriously decorated, and locked gates

and fire within.
I have not changed a great deal

has changed. My moody riverside kingdom
burnt, focal and flightless,

and its deft dead
and their cold, yabbering hearts.

No Dark Pastoral

the sunlight was
different then it
swayed in stalks
like beautiful
blinking sisters
cloaked round in
Eros Eros Eros
I laid the knots of
light down piece
by piece into a
circle there is no
mist-flown field
no great holy
pond of black winds
just the last juice
of March draining
off the board
all my dreams are
wearing bright ugly
waistcoats & it is
spring almost definitely

On Style

A
landscape
requires
precision.
But
a
person.
Spare
me
this
exacting
language
but
leave
to
me
this
godly
weft
it
suits
me
so.

Enemy of the People

What miserable drones and traitors have I nourished and brought up in my household, who let their lord be treated with such shameful contempt by a low-born cleric?

cornered him with three others by the monastic cloister in canterbury cathedral on the twenty ninth of december 1170 & struck him down so the blood was white with the brain & the brain no less red from the blood for the king shot him with a semiautomatic assault rifle for the king poisoned him for the king stabbed him twenty three times for the king the blood was white for the king the brain red for the king did what i was told for the king cut his throat for the king held his head underwater and waited for the thrashing to stop for the king shot him with a high power sniper rifle from the top floor of a bank across the plaza for the king poisoned his pink cocktail at the new years eve party for the king & my country no history of violence but did what the king said for the king long history of domestic violence & sexually violent threats online & did what the king what the king said for the king long history of domestic violence & sexually violent threats online & did what the king said for the king & my country blood was

white & brain no less red for the king
switched out his pills for cyanide for the
king sent bombs to his house for the
king strangled him with a necktie for
speaking against my king for the king
snuck into his house and smothered him
while he slept for the king smashed a
plant pot over his head for the king
turned his blood white with brain and
brain red with blood for the king hanged
him in the garage and framed it as a
suicide for the king shot him through the
heart with an arrow for the king planted
explosives under his car for the king
planted evidence for the king forged
evidence for the king struck him down
for the king struck him down for the king
who is here so vile that will not love his
country cornered him in canterbury
cathedral and struck him down so the
country cornered him in canterbury
cathedral and struck him down so the
blood was white with the brain & the
brain no less red from the blood & the
brain from the blood with the brain & the
brain with the blood was white & red
& blood no less was the brain &
the blood the blood & the brain was
red & white & white was red the
blood no less the blood was red & white
& red & white & red & white & blue

As things stand

resisting lamentation is the height of poetic feeling

we rhyme because we are
animals, troubling quiet with a
treacherous whinnying

"You do that; love me; die alone"

if you would
be the agent
of error this

would not be
the lyric you
were waiting for

touch me soft
often enough
for it to hurt

I am not surprised by men Men do not
surprise me their tools their tacky hearts
their curious girdles Men reckless War
And the smouldering horses

LS003:
OFFICE POEMS

Sarah Fletcher

LEGITIMATE SNACK 003

TITLE: Office Poems
AUTHOR: Sarah Fletcher
Originally printed on:
PAPER: Croxley Heritage Natural White Laid (100gsm)
COVER: Celeste Sirio (290gsm)
ENDPAPER: Marbled Tissue Paper
TITLES: LEMON MILK
TEXT: Blacker Text Book

l run of *40*

"…it's goodbye to lunch to love
to evil things and to the
ultimate good as 'well'"

- FRANK O'HARA, FROM LUNCH POEMS

"Tropical the island breeze
All of nature wild and free
This is where I long to be
La isla bonita"

- MADONNA, LA ISLA BONITA

THE SECOND BETRAYAL, OF COURSE, COMES AS

the disintegration of a 'proven history':

each officiated day
is leapt from rapidly: one quick
immersive island
to the next.

MORE LUCRATIVE THAN SEX

is how (approaching island two)
these pithy operations bleed
in tongues

A newest tongue for every moment
See: 'merger' (which does no flowering)
'touching base' (but so without my hands!)

I am exhausting and efficient
tabling everything

To my love, I am so always
reaching out

LUNCH IS

the day's arrhythmia is
island number five an
abattoir with floors of sand
lunch the lucid dream job
upsetting order's fluency
I send another email menially
consider coffee
eye my deskscape's
little illnesses
I send with every byte
the weight & filth
of a humiliated heart

MONOLOGUE FOR SOLO DUNE

"'The human body' is a terrible magazine

"Strangely circulating

"So many issues

"All day they arrive here, by hand-eye autopilot

"I am where they have chosen to have their thoughts screened out

"Staring into mirages all day...

"At one point something would be real

"Wouldn't it?

"I know them most by what they leave behind

"Pencils, a sweater, columns of uncollected touch"

DESK LUNCH

When I lock eyes with a man
I fold myself into a bill;

I consume the violent foods to balm my mind
And make me more precise;

Veal; offal; any taken baby;
The zest of being twinly-livered, temporarily;

The trick is to identify with it
To make it more delicious;

My tongue lines with a silver sense of dreaming;
One day I will look back to assign intentions;

Colourising photographs of wars.

UNFURLING AHEAD OF ME, NO HIGHWAY OF SAND OR SEA

rather
Uriel's wing
the span of my assigned future
guiding me towards
island (six).

First
I dwell in the exilic ecstasy!

Before the angel steers himself
towards seapoint's mouth.

O co-regent of the sun!
Take me with you! Let me in!

AN EMAIL AND ITS REPLY IS A FLOWER TATTOOED ON A FLOWER

I am against senses entirely: swim, my
puppy-piled heart, or simply
I have been here too long (island seven).

I lap in the gap between my maker
and the one who gives me orders.

Amen: he is so woof
He is productive member
Label inmate

A BRIEF ANSWER TO YOUR QUERY

can be found in the sun's oastic refuse,

whole saunas of loverboys fighting
over who can play a film score
on a single, dinky violin

INSTEAD OF AN EXIT, OR A HALLWAY, THE DOOR OPENS TO FIND

Every swan at St. James Park

Dead from overbreathing in the office Yes my office

Tessellated by the orange tooth on brittle sand

Excitement bejewels too-moving sky, so

Rich with guillotines of fleshy air

an extract from 'CAVIAR'

Beginning again at the
apple's technology,
like an irradiated, video game ninth life,
I eat the juicy fruit - a top-rated, solo, porno-picnic moment,
glittering like the piss of a baby rabbit -
to see its inner workings. Bam. Enter. Swiftly. Thought

LS004:
Bitter Honey

J. H. Prynne

Legitimate Snack 004

Title: Bitter Honey
Author: J. H. Prynne
Originally printed on:
Paper: Tintoretto Gesso (95gsm)
Cover: Woodstock Arancio (285gsm)
Endpaper: Saville Row Tweed Blue (100gsm)
Titles: Bosque
Text: Timeless

1 RUN OF 200 & 1 RUN OF 100

'Covariance: a measure
of the linear dependence
between two random
variables, equal to the
expected value of the
product of their devia-
tions from the mean.'
- Peter Walker,
Dict. of Sci. and Tech.,
1999, s.v.

***

'We know ... that for I
finite the forward and
backward equations
have the same solutions'
- J.R. Norris,
Markov Chains,
Cambridge, 1997, p. 95.

EXEMPT PROVISION

Whereby exempt provision, despite part alternately
fortunate trace to chance, first off receipt ward
deference early and before sound plan, depend on
prior advantage resume hear once the same; in tune
except fine frame galvanise adequate perforate inch
promote esteem, re-open turn or circular back soon
raise vocable spinnaker, seismic towards insisted
luff extreme; take out proposal virtual enough own
elation, time-bound. Deterrent suspect birth limit,
overflow or maxim, comprise infer and so to plead
traffic woven give to level, funnel bird detained
lyre constancy. By rule further stone beyond choice
proof voice logic needful, handful sorrel magic yet
derelict abrasion, sound marker slight; in even but
before provoked mishap, cool after found to play
distended and fraught, in song. By over track in
centre wing, speckled pinion one higher up forever
dismay vein opportune, new work at minimal prolong.

DIVIDE, REMAIN

Or yet random count disquiet fortify pressure inflame
at to for, set miss to edify, palisade. From in search
order lateral axiom ask mere postponed visible task,
nothing out belated or torrid, innovate; fear at least
welcome awaiting, gratitude offence in dilation prune
ambit pasture variant litmus team duet, edge reshuffle
critical annex, pallid reputed to clench forest other
shore. Harbour crescent, rink slavish attachment foil
over prevailing to mix, to flaunt also canvas by final
force erstwhile fanciful ligand parenthood, direct bat
jest you know burn free intuit, dispute. After once or
practical omen ingrained, plant out refinement arrest
will go oblige stannic governance, intubate allege at
front column indifferent. In mercy trial untied, nor
main until redeem brotherhood, total departure entire
consorted faithful jet covert beast foster proemial
inviolate. Avert sustaining prior inductance beladen
ford to bard entrain, allergen missive open film trim
next to last, pervasive less felt else demise obtain.

FLIGHT PATHWAY

Instil bird ride happen inside, imperil fade proceeding minotaur grove expert void. Steel fovea crocus hint or approve collision undeterred proxy moisten yet impute, foremost avian triune illustrious harbinger, brokerage pride enlarge on target box as hurt. Fickle always weird now or than purpose still unheard, drift inflated cousin mirth despite occupy, invite. Relax then, resolve first insulate console probation voided oval vertical chirps eagerly win reclaim nitrogen manual foreign clerk. Date clatter massive braid, alter prominence the whole shot over final conjugate trill racing, affixed detachment cohort pandowy silicon. Intern sublimate modest also, imbricate funded incus fungus reprobate sulphurous fun talon drainage dioptric; alleviating spring fountain neatherd infoiled and address outspan minimal, coronal tactic bearing, strait. Excess provost hindmost crust principle, twitter famous mantle single permanent turn in flock, sky quotient underwrite must to tame choric ambuscade, rip tide grab utter strop invincible. Evensong submerge, perverse cordon reference ignited, all of them emphatic plentiful reduce price tolerant into throat. Redress flotation fibulate cost, on intrinsic trapping, stern beak muster promise isthmus infraction.

ENOUGH CONVERSION

Snap or flit, angle tie to bundle acid subvert, dint twill
mock recover apt sufficient muted. Trim seem intimate caustic
furbish, twitch deserve matching curb block living profile
newel never incriminate, darting elfin cancel seated rowel,
cruel amicable comical destitute. Donates plaque synthetic
immersion, lack impress re-decorate; watch at best sign for
pitch tarnish forensic proof ligate, on deck copper plateau
on resume passamezzo, bin to seem from aid maritime. Or none
distal froward, steward since parlance pursuits to crystal
uncle bowsprit discriminate algae slavery addict inventor
management. Trims back, intact, in front. Purview cataract
wilt cynical dusted, ousted ever or whether totalise open
in franchise allege proper sever improvise. Rephrase lake
anecdote product rash epidote clotted antidote, sad sedge
mischief index hostage to fresh bespoke consent. Yearn in
formal ownership vial claustral glucose unfrozen grasp, to
gasping reticent; fadge alignment confluent dissention at
penitent due forsaken pediment. Outcast in wretch deplete,
servile pledge most sifted, retinue influx sediment confer
flinch continued moss bench; step for touch imprint. Over
rack brunt refuted irrigate dimension, mitosis glamourise
punish fair square livid extracted; converse which tangle
shredded uppermost mulish defence. Lost past first desist.

ANOTHER MORE DENSE

Assuage to wharf daze piste tumbril ooze phantom done
amaze encounter laughing, febrile hostel cladistic in
temperament viscous ascent. Penetrate single planet
foresight half, full-grown awful thimble even snooze
to lose caliph aggressive ensign; disdain. Map wager
sooth grin best, last token leaf ignite affront, net
placid on dauntless transit pavilion, traipse burden
crazing safe. Shaft furnish gainful propose come and
go flounce or riddance, bright rays tremblance mend
over blended. Effort voice treatise boil to furl pit
parrot woken, churlish diction fine payment levitate,
attracted since curtail crest expect saunter privet.
Interpret costume ratten uplift misted pacify generic
holdfast, wrist placed sodden electoral faucet trench
dividend. Forward slight narration trance suspend for
radial join force nurse, previous beaten path; event
if resented amble, modify victory percept terrify at
glowing hearth invest. Crown torment too, silent pat
thrift terse put past vote, saturate enlist native
yet bereft. At last into line promotion town claim
or worse, remit unveil focal hazard retract discover
wasted integrate persistent for different local mint
privation; forensic testify omitted utensil entail
fragmentary culminate. Portrayal gamble glance rend
endemic classical restriction, foisted headway fumble
adaptive tractable predicted, least emollient grain.

EXTEND FORGIVENESS

Offer better admixture, garnish plenish late dacoit
castle missal insufferable, patchwork. Band upwards
tend after, latter admire by choir retention seem
crane rigorous more curious sock depict issuance at
dance yet dance too sweep by troop latch rejoinder;
keep by finder admonish strong down along admirable
for sure endure. Introit collapse at stretch cinder
path thereafter fruit or stitchwort session problem
nutrient relenting absorb orange flange disturbance;
neglect once inspection intern halt quickly by pivot
lack in foster lustre foreign corbel flick invent.
Value press ingested ace to slice parade detox, in
shine box might rejoin by wire brace terminal, twine
assignment effortless near pin restore; sicken wince
aspire floor taps for etch device amnesty imagined
synergy indoor stair breech currency, evince dearly
particulate energy leading to waving, lap implore.
Bactrian footwear entire action station twice over,
fright purloin reign brevet continent, on shoreline
calling vain succession; reduce prolusion missing
extra parts white airlock porous factor profession.
Yield childish action, in sight pince doorway each
win new day; nor seal nor wrinkle singular destruct.

PLAY TO WILL

Forest surgeon makeshift lift-off insertion, sink to bank
frankly poorly brink matter austere merest close avocet
link dewpoint level printed gossip. Mastic gravel tip oil
fiscal ensue proofing headship, outer bludgeon stricken
tank nasal, alter adduce posthumous cut rank; imported
jointed duplex affix roof blanket, caught handed costly
phrasal subject elective to promise limb astute; in dank
deployment interred, sought to swim review too. Do they
will for, dangle ear drops reckon bitten, self infusion
intrinsic prefer loft single damp rill in frost, in front
over lips. Now refute climb uppance itch on sill, proton
twin for them protect mussel binding salt lactic, as weak
intact drastic fortune commune idiot iodine spread fault
deficient. Sound fill address trio handle from ground,
cavern mission imperil melted, into embryo silk patter
filter minded, attended; suited in face ready tracing,
implement rewound ahead, postern entertain not denied,
soloist. Consent then tie front lace success modest toy
to buy, play to will, evident batik scutcheon transfuse
relief opportune. You soon all shall final appended, wend
degree to cut free, for but season; moulted far forward
by optic muse. Serve cruise in place border reason foison
catch in throat distended; high-jinks larynx bite impend.

OWL TO MAPLE

But once out to reach, tarnish instead gilded up lurch
blench antagonise, yawn over firm to negligent announce
famish; dispraise olive occupy dissident procured fitted
ounce omit jetty munch few to chew, amazing harness rend
redound to swallow accent, clemency; that too, burnish
complete tread optimum, invective in wild unsold. Skipper
late ocellated squint perverse trinket in furnace, knee
argus stroll mildew, spawn in season. Legal counterpart
friction mental comprised, before insure coloured, if in
teach first; revise surrogate early dawn, ichor clouds
unfold. Prize tenancy freed as few line careworn, brown
ensue gain solution. Ingrain mallow follow yell, steal
banish; go to, anon, discern together rowan mountains.
Bright good flood scrubland, ought, tenter fret disguise
polymerase micro unlit, untorn. Gone in peach provided,
mellow how many qualify, primate frustrated percentile
datum; pinny frenzy mended, tune stubborn melt astride,
skim. Sardine prince qualm. Trait mutton blame, yielded
outlandish wanton, thorny tantrum overmuch. Guess tiff
brazen ivy, borrow nor lend, sand castle. Shine twain
in cloud, hidden and lazy, salt lock birds in glory,
attenuate bestowed. Praise nowhere by the wood, carry
add yolk why not; pilchard forward enucleate ride in
front, praline symmetric ebonised, chronicle refrain.

SO AFTER ANOTHER

Wick stop in power transience, reduction portion saving
ahead damage foot speck, elbow vantage bisque. Nervous
landless per crooked district, ample to cramp, oven first
truce lenient prowl ancient step-fast fund. Lick enhance
forage will engagement, licit banter ferment, crescent
set better for butter, nervous admission. On disc raffish
behaviour cornice, up to or through, anvil gravity select
effusive heat penitent after fact, under temple deducted
crypt. Brachial on lintel, curls dented over brew, slip-
ware molten zig-zag saturate refract furnace. Crevice,
lichen plaint arabesque birth canal amended surplice in
surplus ingrate, countable deficit traffic pliancy front;
usual late polite exonerate darling, win to drag or fend
to stamp, lassitude. Whose stock derail uncoil selfishly
brush deturned, scapular lavish sprain, rise to ingest
tropic restive, furthest in virgin flight. All watching
affrighted costed indolent, risk terse pact infertile,
and still they tell crudely tangent overall remaindered.
Desertion for winter-light numeral obvious plural, insert
accurate, astute. Sustenance near coincident: manna from
haven snow given shrewdly reserved bipolar surge allow.
So many company appoint in split pin anodyne, sumptuary
apposite undistorted, all asunder version white enteric
regime proclaim incorporate; amend, distraught, protect.

WALL GERMINATE

As here to be firm storm, to see from suit worn despite
span over flighted, in spate fury, return; rage by fire
torn sky-patch shudder, esperance accrue, open heaven
founder awed inform dilate returning, passage old swim
near sight line composite, cloud riven score. Recruit
list tempest crack, vertebrate cluster avertive delink
astonish blast contended; insistent violate calming
fissure rip-well, offer to scrape tabulate destruction
imminent. Back to stand redound cretic billow, by wore
ravage, punish underset crash of waters next in black,
struck face depicted; ever for, rock groin as pitiful
thunder, odious wrack partition as unknown, below wait
debated, derelict. Transit plunder narrow deluge midge
frangible, obligate, racket surmounted vatic diminish
rush to judge. Nominate inroad crustal, lateralised
washout grievous antic, over take cover in severance
undercoat. Further spoilt averted, tilt formaldehyde
explosion invented as crush to blame, profane parlance
sideways, fluent slanted currency in torrent format.
Falsetto whistle boasted might perforate, impersonate
incised reproof dank coverlet militia; soon out remit
by prior merciful reprieval investment. Onyx crash
both porous, soak to floated, muted on tip rejoinder.

LS006:
COLOURING BOOK

Wayne Holloway-Smith

Legitimate Snack 006

Title: Colouring Book
Author: Wayne Holloway-Smith
Originally printed on:
Paper: Constellation Snow Tela Fine (130gsm)
Cover: Lampone Sirio Colour Card (290gsm)
Endpaper: White Translucent Vellum (100gsm)
Titles: Palatino Linotype
Text: Noto Serif

1 run of 50

The red lobster's beauty only comes out when it's dropped

I get the feeling I'm about to be born and can't
I am a heart that's beating against the borders
                              of every room
now the shadows are retreating

remove the frames or the lines of their edges
and they grow
like spilling water –

we hold ceremonially our fingers
and shrink to the point of not
knowing (Oh excellent Magpie)

the earth will swallow us
but not yet not yet –
until the fear passes I am going to speak

the length of my body:
I have just two hands the feeling of the world
and a confession to make: wait –

it sticks like a lump in you
but you swallow it just the same
I breathe I breathe – ok: now:

at the bottom
of everything
is a hallelujah

              ~

the signifier is always continuous
and slow good pain –
only in time itself is there room

the red lobster's beauty only comes out when
                                 it's dropped
the mornings of the last fine days
are the freshest – most limpid (Magpie)

and the apples are being gathered
the crickets are screaming bloody Thursday
                           and the sky
everywhere animals disappear – they look
                              sideways
"you don't seem to be happy"
"oh yes I am happy but I am sad" and the earth

will swallow us but not yet –

to go back to the original hunger was impossible
it was not real yet –
and with such profound joy

I was trying to finish
the poem before
your nails dry

~

near the kettle autumn was advancing –
so swollen at the churn
still – at the tub and ironing board

the following will illustrate the losing of objects
up and singing   broken
contemplating what to have for dinner

everything is a hallelujah
a bunch of clothes I wanted to buy on the internet
a tooth an odd fragment

I was low and shaken strained out of myself
content to accept as a free gift what the earth
and showers had given

one fork one cup
one shoe one sock
a vego bar every time I finish a page

of a colouring book I immediately grasp
the hidden sense of this
symptomatic action

another
pointless talent
I'm unveiling

~

I was trying to finish the poem before your nails dry

my amygdala needs to find its calm place –
I literally yelled your name out the window

to go back to the original hunger was impossible
a stomach rocking as a baby rocks
beyond what's beyond thought

pushed back by voices and lullabies and bribes
autumn advancing one fork one shoe at a time
like I asked a direct question or clocked something

only what destroys can be told (Magpie)
I have just two hands the feeling of the world
and a confession to make:

this is a love poem
this is a love poem
for someone I'm not yet allowed to love

the park closed and the woman locked
the green gates before we could
have sex on the fresh stone

beneath which
lay a rotted
William Blake

Notes and Acknowledgements

This poem is made of bits of directly cited, spliced or slightly altered texts, fragments of WhatsApp messages and moments of my own invention.

Texts include

Agua Viva by Clarice Lispector
The Nature of the Universe by Lucretius trans. R.E. Latham
The Philosophy of Andy Warhol by Andy Warhol
Beloved by Toni Morrison
Psychopathology of Everyday Life by Sigmund Freud
Why Look at Animals by John Berger
The Immoralist by André Gide
A Lover's Discourse by Roland Barthe

LS006.1:
COMIC BOOK

Margot Holloway-Smith

&

Wayne Holloway-Smith

Legitimate Snack 006.1

Title: Comic Book
Author: Margot Holloway-Smith
&
Wayne Holloway-Smith
Originally printed on:
Paper: Constellation Snow Tela Fine (130gsm)
Cover: Lampone Sirio Colour Card (290gsm)
Endpaper: White Translucent Vellum (100gsm)
Text: Handwriting

1 run of 20

I
WANT-
ED
TO
TELL
YOU
SOME-
THING
BEAU-
TIFUL
SO
I
DID

YOUR HAIR FALLING DOWN LIKE ASTRONAUTS FROM SPACE

WHEN
WAS
THE LAST
TIME
YOU
CLICKED
YOUR
FINGERS
AND A CANDLE
DIDN'T
LIGHT

IT FEELS LIKE A BIRTHDAY PARTY WATCHING YOU DRAW

WHEN WE PLAY MUSICAL STATUES ALWAYS YOU WIN Do you not

"DADDY"

IS

A

DOUBLE

ARO-

DUS-

TTE

ON

MY

CHEST

TISSUE

LS007:
Voss

Imogen Cassels

Legitimate Snack 007

Title: _Voss_
Author: Imogen Cassels
Originally printed on:
Paper: Sirio Color Perla (80gsm)
Cover: Freelife Vellum White (215gsm)
Endpaper: Banana Thai Tissue - Sea Grey (45gsm)
Titles: Big Caslon
Text: Garamond

2 runs of 50

Demain, dès l'aube
after Victor Hugo

The Mains—a lobe—or hour where I blanch almonds in fizz
    (oh day), and you will party and we'll wait for one another
    all bone and grace. Back from green foray to undo
    or cleanse with snow. Now Cupid's inspiring the plants
    with love again. I can't stay dying like a far-off
    lentil any longer, rue comet.

Chéri for leisure fixate on me in heartful discomposes or some
    bell untrust: the window will mean nothing, I'll not know
    flora but the light changed when you and everything has
    different motives nowhere. Making my trinity against
    the doe with all her thorns and holy fennel, sadly. I don't
    know how it got there; a cat, grafting for happiness, dark glasses.

The skies stony or subjunctive with grief I won't see them
    or the distantagain where your love I broke a glass out of
    and look at green Harfleur. Its late roses. I'll really tell you,
    someday, metrically, another tomb, and rev of getting tight
    on gin or just dull *spero*—a handful towards holly, heath air,
    flowers, love's last known movements, a star a star—

Technicolour in silk
after W. S. Graham

in glass's coastline, costume, or
painted-on—a swan washing itself
at night. Triolet as if to rhyme

with little flower, or any architrave
for itself. How lazy. Your long
thin draughts, walking across

a heaven. Anyhow and way
the white-daubed windows dwell
privately, in the morning,

on the premise of snow or whether
its petals. The heart moves anyway,
I mean, whether it is moved. *Holding*

the wolf in chace. Farfetched as love
as a fox outwitting the hounds. Where
rose jam falls up into technic.

[Party-cranes circuit-board blood-sugar.]
What shall I send you? The animals
whose skins we live in; a patch of dark

that's barbed or smoking-out the image;
bloodstrike and irreversibly open my wrists
all over senate house lawn. Smiling

because I'm with you without anything
repaired. By which I mean to say, that is
YOU BASTARD WHERE ARE YOU which is love

so much implied
for NS

nate rosadog nail she'll work or chew on buck sage
crying *yeah yeah*. the santal corner better shiver
in its sparkplug, bright eyed with something. you
come out reading without made of tears; the ring
and green man. along me darling bound like a skin
fluke as amethyst or marble bluejohn—we're o new
build heron and the sedge like a prairie raccoon dog
fox fucking whatever. as if it might turn out this time
and fall to some grand jeté but as ever underwater;
know I make a habit of its matter. that I love
the tiercel his un-blue streak of recognition fastened
darkly to futility, this long move out into the sun.

Say I am you
Suilven—Achiltibuie

Honey—no /// salt, a
    pleasure principle—of foxes.

    July in Scandi-gothic ore
a jellyfish suspended darkly in vers;

sum Cimabue-type relief my
    kinch brothers climbing

    a hill, with gold-in-black scotch.
I love you / are not here it is very

boring, & even I do nothing so well
    as you. Achmelvich strive / Stevie's

    fashion slant disliking the angle
of her hat: where earth comes apart

from ground: the world quietly
    adjusting itself in its own sights.

    our subjunctive history, in beauty and in trees:
how bitter comfort is, how unwelcome saints.

after Bhanu Kapil

i

Dear animal   dear skull adorned with freesias
I've been absent   my hip-at-lift   the veille
Rocked by a magnet   or your voice   that's womb alone
To court a star   or sable   further than fluid
Dove-breasted   an eyelash shining   to a rib
Held up by love   moving in the wake of my lap
And hot walk   on the hill   beyond a mother
Horses whickering   to bitter rose   clutched to a hold
Island assumption   pond-eyed burning   after ambiguity
For help   dear translation—
                              Where is the beginning?

ii

Rain makes for fine dust, neat, cold and semi-luminous
as shot spirit. I have hinged upon myself, with anterior
motive, after a gory pantone meniscus, brushing outwards.
O sever: this hazard as danger or luck, the reason I existed
faded to catskin, one morning as early as it was late.
Finding the index in design for easy hunting; the rung
of the forest floor, cloven oakmoss, blood and cistus.
I looked up my sharp old register for a collar or trim
and found myself—through the whole mist—home,

x settlements in the direction
of the beginning

To write down everything about the world would be impossible,
    why bother; this piece of work, unlike some better ones,
has no sense of the inevitable: so no end.
You must take the film off things, or maybe glaze, to catch them,
    else they are not still enough. Reported sightings of a white hart
far across the continent.   Red soak.
I loved the party, all upper smoke and apples.
    I don't care—go eat gravel, occupy houses, walk the night,
shut
yourselves out on the roof, summer in drained bathtubs.
    The heart being our automatic—
        (Now that is some Good Blood.)
    Take no love for granted.
        Take no love for granted.
This 'proposal to "live the body—Untitled, is our plough, all
    to where the poem may be quietly hurtling, under the sky-coloured
sky, before an outer dark.
Asking what exactly is the dusk intuition of writing for *one Spring
day*,
    shortly before your death in Autumn, where you are kept.
How did you know. And all this struggling for grace
    which troubles me, three white stones beyond analysis.
These kind of dives go pretty deep, a word or two before you go
with flexion in apology, rage at fly-pasts, quite salvaging

after Dom Hale

against the tiny rivulets of chance—
and preference being tacit—
this perfection
                    of voss & razorclams,
you aleph, or bunch

                         of nacreous buttons,
namely my own. all this in praise,
at least, of simple movement:
     a set of angels at chess.
the hart (that dimpled thing) directed
via leylines, a pair of obliques

pulling south like bells. a rung. oh
my lightfoot you windfucker you
furious excuse for a buzzcut.

quiet in my little diamond collar like a bride
at her second wedding, on her third
small glass of red wine, swaying
                                        this will be

and sighing
                                        if the spirit moves me

there's a hare dripping blood in the corner
well, we shared a city, didn't we?
we once knew the same weather

LS008:

The Pictures of my Youth

Richard O'Brien

Legitimate Snack 008

Title: The Pictures of My Youth
Author: Richard O'Brien
Originally printed on:
Paper: Acquerello Bianco (100gsm)
Cover: Pastel Blue Plain (160gsm)
Endpaper: Neon Kiwi Green (80gsm)
Titles: Catull
Text: Segoe UI

2 Runs of 50

hello.jpg

All eyes converge on that red bloom
just right of centre, lipgloss-bright:
the hearth of a dull room, a tuna steak
served bloody on that sickly pale ruched back.

Strong hands distend the hole like theatre curtains:
from raised veins, the intensity of clutch
is palpable. The dick and balls seen *verso*,
hoisted taut: almost an afterthought.
Thighs bulge towards a corrugated wallpaper,

and once you heard his name was Kurt or Kirk,
he'd displayed himself for a hundred shots like this;
didn't know for sure that this was one of his.

It shut down *Soul Stories* on Oprah's forums, iced
a readers' comments feature for the *L.A. Times*,
and still somehow took five full years to fall foul
of the Christmas Island internet authorities.

Now the domain claims to be selling
cryptocurrency, a Russian mirror all
that's left of what — that gaping, grouper mouth —
we can now recognise as manifesting
a certain democracy of spread.

No one's too young to suffer

Still live, although you're instantly diverted
to pop-up chatrooms, adverts for Cialis,

this is all it is: three old men on plumped bedding,
sheets white, bodies pressed so close

they barely trace the outline of a triangle.
One of them, with the mutton chops

and silvered parting of a fifties action star,
kisses the baldest of the set, palm flush

to his right nipple. Furred forearm to elbow:
this, and the formal headboard, and his partner's cock

the only verticals — this last snug in the mouth
of Old Man #3, whose sharp nose shadow-strokes

the first man's balls, his hair time-tonsured
to a halo with a cockatiel's quiff.

Two clouds of dusted pubes merge in the blur,
and all is tender, all seems orderly —

what straight lace-curtain sentimentalists
might call 'Love In Old Age', though we can't say

it's love, or how what lives they've lived
have brought them here, the far side of an awful century,

to this Nataraja of limbs, flesh almost sutured,
and so if we must intrude, let's only say:

when you are old and grey and full of cum,
may there be many mornings like this one.

I remember the whole thing being rotated 90° to the right

Her marble-glossy flesh
the whitest thing on show — wedged in that boxy tub,
its popcorn-husk, witchetty-grub
shade counterpoints her calf-socks, and the flash

of vomit-orange which erupts,
as if out of a water-bed uncapped,
from that pink pucker. Though she's trapped,
that spiralling tornado coils and bucks,

its high-aspiring plume
shooting beyond the frame, before it arcs back:
helix, cataract,
like melting salted caramel ice cream

onto her crushed black hair,
surgical mask, staining the heels and toes
she clutches as in yoga pose —
and you might think she'd been abandoned there

in her cascading filth,
her actions' consequences, were it not the case
that someone laid a silver gauze
mat neatly underneath her head. The stealthy

angle of the shot betrays
a care in composition: how the round, curved
ass observes the rule of thirds —
the left side soft, right straight, that central spray

the focus of our gaze.
Someone has blurred her vulva, introducing
a quaint modesty, sparing
the barest blushes. We don't know who paid

for this billowing moment,
nor can we assume its meaning to those screened eyes.
All we bring is our surprise
that mounts, and troubles only in descent.

1,727

eternal loop the dead   androgynous
pop singer   compares   his baby to
a record for   the number of spins   was set
by four students   in Ireland   evidence is
hard becondomed cock   thrusts   nimbly up
on rocking thighs   on black-and-white
striped area around   the upper crotch
the tan-shy outline where   a thong would be
dick swinging anticlockwise   and the whole
effects of porn on young   viewers remain
hard becondomed cock   thrusts   numbly up
bodies converge like accordion ribs   and still
point at the centre of the spinning world   is this
trimmed bush   the counter climbs   rewarding
stamina after a while   a neat grey box assigning
my identity   is complicated   if
a dick spins   in a forest   no one there to
see it   hear it   see it   hear it   see
it's posited that all our lives cohere/jump in one

Fructify

after the anthropologist came home
from an exhibition she noticed
a very strange rash and quickly dismissed it
believing the Holes would leave in time
and she was given Antibiotics and special creams
she sought help from a more certified doctor
unfortunately the doctor was on vacation
she removed the bandages to find
Larvae squirming in the pores and sores
sometimes these wicked creatures would
all together simultaneously move around
into different crevices the fat tissue
the milk canals even deeper than she had
originally thought our undergarments are made
all over the world they sit in boxes
go through many hands and exchanges
we do not know what parasite in our clothes
crawling teeming for instance read the article first
preferably in boiling hot water the seeds in flesh
a genuine injury most commonly found in Asia
98.9% of people watch the pods peep out
like meerkats now even the green root
looks suspicious the only difference
the background hard instead of pink
skin-softness each beaded sphere arranged
concentrically plenty of room around them
cupped in gentle hands you feel your own
breast tense as if licked by a rough tongue

sometimes a more ragged colony an archipelago
of dots of buds a thriving cave system
where messages * **you'll never use shampoo
again** * are passed from mouth to mouth
in the dim fires of the night.

LS010:

Each Sharper Complication

Kyle Lovell

Legitimate Snack 010

Title: Each Sharper Complication
Author: Kyle Lovell
Originally printed on:
Paper: Illusion Parchment Alpine White (100gsm)
Cover: Antracite Sirio Colour Card (290gsm)
Endpaper: Woodstock Arancio Paper (110gsm)
Titles: Trade Gothic Next SR Pro
Text: Arno Pro

1 run of 50

Waking Theory

Imagine beautiful and exhausted companies
of dancers of lifeguards of accountants
with their ticked-off pay rolling out the sky

Is this the beginning of course not there is
still so much for a handful to do in losing a finger
before the work of a real society can begin

So over time and again over worked I dreamt
of automation theories that discussed the waking
labour of waking up and interpreting sunshine

On my last partner's face the sky had called it quits
the conditions were unfeasible and culminating in general
strikes against my happiness and I'm not a scab

But at my worst I'm in love with cruising in straight times
through the suburbs of pragmatic gays who invested wisely
in the right areas of legislation of their city of their poems

Where they have double beds so imagine beautiful
exhausted me in the arms of someone who hated someone
and let me work out the theory of waking up here

Samphire Hoe

Left a sprig of samphire on the warm stone
as dreadful trade, and left with my head half-
hung low. I lost too much to chalk it up
as the general movement of the grey-fire waves
wetting a set of partially worded sandals.
Now, I recognise that there's no set path down
this Dover beach, only seaweed and stone

to remark a turn onto Samphire Hoe.

Warehouse Song & Song

debt's brisk banality
come on now
keep those black torches up
we're still growing
with each working day
it's only a red searchlight
now sleeves now cuffs
now belt now beanie
just in case you love
all these objects
a little too much
we have you covered
please don't worry
we have you covered
as the rain or ink blots
dropping in expected
unable to pay for
the language is
as language does
all it can
on a delayed bus
routing around for work
it's all too long
too fervent
too too

now jump
shout and jump
to wither this ghost
through its vine
wily as a fox
cornered and beaten
copper helmet and pan
please understand
I am talking about ethics here
about those early shifts in time
the ambience of hand-dryers
hese broken cubicle locks

Wincheap Repetition

Refolding immediate loves into sheet metal,
can I offer you a long-term warranty on that burnishment?

Excessive polishing is just as bad as inattention,
though that's aesthetics for you, getting all caught up in a typo.

I've been as artificial as the next son-of-a-bastard
& drunk as him too. After all, you caught my latest batch

of drifting nightly through these penny arcades.
It's romance, it's romance, it's an ode about romance.

Technical Notes on Mishearing

What love doesn't beyond you?
           Each industrial desire line pylons

behind my garden. It's not hidden,
           it's just this summer reiterating that

within an infinite universe, defeat
           is always inevitable, but so also is victory.

So hold us close to your favourite heart
           and read us aloud in your favourite pub,

we'll stay in a constant state of whelm
           but you'll get used to it after this last

season spent in another state
           of being in a park at a protest

of a failure of a tear
           of a cherry tree that spits its seeds

into my favourite poem
           that you will read into a friend's mouth.

Each month and Monday always
        intends to pass on that inherent once

more time passes, but we've
        got Stendhal's radio in here and it tells me

how she's coping with all of this.
        When you spend a year in the middle

of love it's difficult not to crack
        the plaster of a Holiday Inn here.

Welcome biped, we're screwing up
        our harmony, our compasses misaligned.

In This Moment

all materials abound
& so we materialise
his wings bent back
by these thumbtacks
as the clause tightens
& twigs are drawn close
with rapt wire round his beak
& suddenly it's the manner
of hermeneut economics
as to which way his feathers singe
beneath allium bulbs
all royal in tender light
& we note that he burns with grace
when becoming horizontal
& when becoming weight

or less in the cross sight

Sincerely Compassionate You

I sincerely compassionate you folding
like a lyric reflux; you mistook an I for an eye
and now there's little but love to play with.

Though where's the reader in all of this?
We must imagine they're sat beside us with a soft grin
and a handful of unnumbered pages,

as they're tendering to give us all
the wrong information. Though to be honest,
we couldn't be any happier about it.

The Church of St. Peter and St. Paul, Uppingham

for C

To busy ourselves with joy -
        that's what song
        (and you are such a song)
        is for.

Notes to the pamphlet and poems

The pamphlet's title is taken from R.F. Langley's 'The Gorgoneion' in Collected Poems, ed. Jeremy Noel-Tod (Carcanet, Manchester, 2015, p. 49).

'Samphire Hoe' draws upon William Shakespeare's description of a Dover cliff in King Lear: 'The crows and choughs that wing the midway air / scarce so gross as beetles; halfway down / hangs one that gathers samphire, dreadful trade!'

The italiscised lines in 'Technical Notes on Mishearing' are lifted from Sean Bonney's 'Comets & Barricades: Insurrectionary Imagination in Exile' in All This Burning Earth: Selected Writings of Sean Bonney (Ill Will Editions, 2016, p. 23).

'Waking Theory' and 'In This Moment' were originally published in marlskarx and Blackbox Manifold.

LS011:
Two Odes

Dom Hale

Legitimate Snack 011

Title: Two Odes
Author: Dom Hale
Originally printed on:
Paper: Woodstock Betulla (110gsm)
Cover: Coral Pink Card (300gsm)
Endpaper: Gold Fleck Xuan, off-white
Titles: Arno Pro
Text: Goudy

1 run of 50

TO BE HONEST

for the tourists

I am your secret hornet. Are they collapsing,
Billions? The price of something tanks.
Minute taking in a hazmat suit
My fifth living gets battered, pavilion for silver
Though estranged, nonscarce. Table service. Keyhole perjury.
Pass me the cheaper bottle, vector. All bets off.
And fending for itself, our lone canard the linnet
Commits a song to bladdered meadows,
Wayward feels the sun, while in a pinch and seawise,
Deposits railing against the T&Cs, I've
Had it with ornate disgust. Theoretically. Get
In the car. The thing about war crimes is
Irrelevant to our web developers. A module
To trust, and microchipping regal. A perfumed star.
What matters is how we tell our tale again,
How to keep a lookout, though winded, winged
Sandals dodging tranches of heroic mist.
And, in the plague state, the subjunctives of
Liberal narration manhandle everyone.
Tough shit. I am fucking perilous. I am
Butting and heretical, the default Podunk
Subtitle. Get this, luckless: a subsidiary of the crater
Hits the spot. It's rigged. Incriminating bends

A kingdom arc of photocopies, bothered coworker,
But what about the Lehman Sisters?
The financialization of the oesophagus. Opera and
Mishap. Rhetoric and dieback. Poetry and centrism.
Then AstraZeneca pelt up to the dock.

And you think it's history that hates you?
The gale blows over international waters
Without purpose, and you are near me
As the satellites are not. This was our backup objective,
To speak all havoc, wrest a gleaming breastplate
From the scamps. Because the melody of the correct
Is fabulous in joylessness, a set of ornamental daggers
For the equations worked out earlier.
I salute it, but it's not for me. You'll be sorry
To the tune of evidence-based spindrift
When the systems analysts deign one day to tweak us,
Cropped to shit. A multistorey car park that
Commences in one century, terminating in another.
Not that the McDonald's was open yet.
And is it guileless to earmark being beautiful?
No more echoing in potholes, no more
Heeding what they pressure you to write.
Rattled still, and snaking grimly through an institution
We despise, the effort to insist on movement's
Always brittle, profession without end. You don't say.
Take another ogle of the Broad Street pump.

Messengers zigzag the lower layers, no fun
For the higher-ups or the rump insurance payments
Of the Ancien Régime. A queue of disembodied questions
Looks to be rebuking you. That's just Monday.

Golden the end is nigh, the enemy is
Time itself. Which room for the plenary again?
Repugnance to imagine the exit streak
Of all minimising invoices. But here's a
Tearful sidebar anyway. Not idle is the wrath of state,
Tolerably bankrupt. Pick a sector. Pick a sphere.
The architectonics are those of freedom, the butcher
Is spangled and fresh from IT. Then soldier on boldly,
Back into the sauna. The trickle-down has
That booze stink. Rentier is not a religion
But it might as well be. So put a mortal sock in it.
Our full cohesion with events managers everywhere.
And that's all from the carsick legislator. A welcome
Distraction. Blow the parsonage.

ON NAÏVE AND SENTIMENTAL POETRY

Stop yakking. They'll cotton on yet.
We love the colour coral, punch-drunk on the
UHT of paradise, and I've got one foot firmly sowed
In the cruelty of baroque conditions as they stand,
The other planted with a sinuous dedication
On the bright auxiliaries. We'll be hying round the panel
When we come, with garlands in our outgrown hair,
A living ocean by the back pocket and no end
To skylit triumphs or the daring escapades
Of midsummer. The audacity, a feel
For strawberry, feats gracing the taste buds
Before melting into an unread email,
A fable from the mucky pups, my finest archers,
Familiar aroma of deluxe descent. Illegal chaos, ours.
I will never be sensible; you will never be proper:
Between us this might just frame a way of doing things.
The agents of atrocity fret before the deep
Azure and backstabbers embezzle every pill.
Their CEO performs a sacrifice onboard
A grounded Boeing jet, but Tooting Market
Has a charm for me. Your music is the insolent kind
And it was ever thus, the wilful contradiction

Of governing necessity, yet nonchalant
As a starling on the open palm of the lollipop worker.
So do it, rise up from the ricks. Get on your feet.
We can cross now, sweetheart, if you take my arm:
Our luck will raze the sane malicious sky.

I'm sobbing in my dressing gown again.
Show up for me. Poetry will be the whole shebang.
We walk the unbelieving streets. I know
The watchword of the nonpareil.
You yank me back from the abyss.
And do not for one second listen
To that drivel on the timeline, damaged
Hierarchies of the righteous. Ignore those wounded
Who calculate a fresh career move in their grief.
This is a penchant for my cherished troubadours,
Streamlined sele, swimming with delight, vicarious in truth,
Strung anciently, big as a billboard. But I'm filthy,
Always had a magpie's eye, throwing riffs and voices
In a frenzy over the caryatids. Back in a jiffy
From the balcony, ruffled plasma screen,
In two ticks of a sphinx's tail. Hit return.
Obviously you can't just brainstorm for the food
Riot. It has to be spontaneous as wildfire.
And it's okay to miss your people, let them be,
Set them right, watch them fail. It's alright to launch
The full abundance of yourself into a grazed

Outgoing atmosphere. Indulgent negativity wipes
Clean off the phone. I'm all out of riddles
But I'm really on one now. Clinking glasses,
A melodious scheme, one tremble in the weather pattern
Dominating over there. Pitch a UFO or frisbee
Through cerulean sprays, just don't
Run out of steam. I know I've been behind you,
Tripping over my belongings to catch up.
Well here's another wager, boys. Here's
A bouquet for the next world, something sweet,
Unalloyed. I turn in fury and dissatisfaction
To the objects of my life, a card trick
Up the sleeve. No skyscraper stays vertical forever,
The fields are ripe with battle, I tip
Out of my hammock and the rest is seized.

We get it, it's over, we must pack up our things.
The councillors of multimurder take the floor.
They say it's only inevitable that I should pass away,
And soon, scattered singing to the waterfalls of wicked data,
Systematic misery. And yet with a hand on my hip
Utopia is everywhere in evidence: to feel it
Is to hold ourselves. Everyone awash with promise
By the ragged rainbow. For I've got the hang
Of how to look through contradiction
Not as something to be abjured, rescinded
In the veils of social night, but as a floodlight

On our weltering in place, a fusee in the whirlwind,
Pendant of activity through hating days.
Such bank statements shouldn't have been possible,
Not now, with endless grinding bullshit to ingest,
Every other interaction just a headache to avoid.
Still, it doesn't have to be this way. The International
Space Station is gladly out of reach, glimpsed
Barefoot from Blackpool beach, as we drift
Together, payout of further spiel. And therefore
These are counter-messages to contract or shirk,
Announcers of distorted spring. Nod in the
Spiralling street, when the sun keeps like a dandelion clock
Low on the horizon. A dead cert. There they go
In the green shiel. To love is like an asymptote.
So much is taken away that something has to give.
Does it hurt like it used to? Do I slur?
You're my best friend, lullay,
Walking home to work.

May 9 2020

LSO13:
Crescent Earth

Astra Papachristodoulou

Legitimate Snack 013

Title: Crescent Earth
Author: Astra Papachristodoulou
Originally printed on:
Paper: Munken Lynx Rough (90gsm)
Cover: Tintoretto Black Pepper (250gsm)
Endpaper: Celestial Astro Vellum
Titles: Obviously
Text: Ebrima

1 run of 30

innermost
from Mercury

floating terrace
far, but so close
on the edge of
solar shoreline

for unchange

from Jupiter

365 million miles
between me & you
to mark discretion

as a drifter, blown
far from you, yet
you're always there

telos is the horizon
from Sun

   O u think me eternal
O a borrowed view
   O triggering a new
O finality into that
   O off-centre blue-green
O before us you grow
   O homeward nearness

anticipatory
from Venus

spins slowly but now
moves like forward
inhaled in the breath
edge-keeper of haze
you exude attraction

counterfuture
from Mars

you speak of futurity
and potential elsewhere
I speak of inaction
tearing you to almost
certain emergency

momentary

a rare pendulum
from Saturn

seeing Earth is like
seeing another focus
making & unmaking,
unfinished nature
woven inside a sphere
of hanging light

mosaico
from Uranus

spinning,
spinning pulse
twist – and dance
around the curves
it seeks refuge

metamorphoses
from Neptune

moving earth-fields
caught in moving blue
moment to moment
lands caught in manic
rage of moving blue
earth-drifts the planet
earth-shines the green
concrete blue-drifts
creating momentum

LS014:
haemorrhage

Aaron Kent

Legitimate Snack 014

Title: Haemorrhage
Author: Aaron Kent
Originally printed on:
Paper: Munken Lynx Rough (90gsm)
Cover: Tintoretto Cubeba (250gsm)
Endpaper: Stargazer Cotton Candy Vellum
Titles: Palatino Linotype
Text: Palatino Linotype

1 run of 30

A Little Wisp of Soul

I am sleeping in the boatman's hideous wake
on the River Styx again,
the frenetic tide a magnet
for every timid soul resorting to its own drowning.

In the earliest hours
I have allowed spirits inside our room
To reluctantly haunt me back to full health
and a welcome state of mind.

It is my resolve that I live to see my bleeding brain
burst into cerebral fireworks
behind my fresh eyes
as the doctors release stubborn dye
into the core of me.
We can examine the results in suspension
and call it either luck or circumstance.

I have nothing left to offer anybody
except the gentle framing of recovery.
When it is time to leave I will use a wheelbarrow
to transport these heavy bones, to carry the old
cartilage I have given away to protect my matured habits
that have driven me to the edge of heaven

as suburbia as a new solitude.
The late march death march will be easier
as a little spirit bearing up a corpse

Clock Genes

There are six circadian rhythms
Between a fundamental loss of the day's glow
And keeping time removed in a petri dish.

It is an expression of my weakness for you
that I am withholding sleep
to cradle your definition
in spite of the physiological arousal
I ingest as lacrimal acidic rain.

Each night I consider filing an application
for the position of my own
professional mourner,
so if circadian rhythm finds me
loose as ash pirouetting beside streams
I will know how to spell my name
tattooed with a bic upon your clavicle.

Is it too late to cognitively label me as grief
And batten down the funeral rites
For an exercise in pre-emptive mourning.

An Experiment in Material Redundancies

At midnight I used to count small mercies
along the perpetual sandman has left dust
in the corner of the room again. We have
asked for it to be sieved like loose leaf

tea into our eyes, delicately so as not to
interrupt suburbia is a place in hell. The
radiator is always set on high and I am
living vest to vest in in effort to control

this sweat but you love the gloss of rain
against my is that the time? I am watching
clocks instead of sleeping, a habit bore
into me through superstition it may kill

night is torture. I've slept once before
and it was everything you spoke of, all
translucent vellum guillotined to fit today's
architecture. Can we spend tomorrow

measuring every moment so I have
a catalogue to wear me like a gown
on a cold morning and tell me you love
me in ways dreams could never express

Midnight Elegy

This brain has become the very symbol
of determining how to sleep with the
mice eating our insulation. It's cute now,
sure, but how's it going to feel ice-drenched
in winter as the calcium has made
your bones so brittle they come home to

my last dance as a matador. Obviously
I couldn't flash the crimson target due
to both my lapse of judgement and
bring me back to states of arousal.
You don't understand. I have earnt
these headaches by glistening my

weight in earthy aromas. By bench pressing
a reputation in the throes of Father.
There he is again, popping up like
a stroke pops up and ends the lucky
streak you had avoiding life-changing
into and out of a werewolf when the full

death rattle, at least that's what I think
they call it. Emma tells me I have to
learn not every man is a father figure
is a lot to take in. I haven't seen myself
in fifteen days now, but I still know
how big the blood clot is, and what

a thunderclap headache feels like should
I find myself staring down the barrel
of the acupuncture isn't helping. I've
grown to enjoy a pain I can set my watch
by, so every week I pay to let my neighbour
prick me like a symbol of a hemorrhage

A God Counting Jinxes

If we're really slipping in and out of
hourglasses, then I suppose we should
cross our arms and hope to space between
us. I don't think there's a crop duster

in the upstairs apartment collecting
my assumptions, listing tiny omens
in my feeding tube is empty. Having
a catheter removed is a whole new

level of saw a charcoal-black fox.
It purred redemption as we drove
south for the winter, arguing whether
foxes purr or wait for melancholy

to harmonise with the ultrasound
night. I hear it sleeping on the ward,
a low hum beating like the sky God
playing a new drum. I think it wakes

when we're silent as grotesque
architects to heaven; I know it counts
our jinxes. I know it wants me to pray.
I have nothing to offer but a phone-call

home declaring a date for my return,
a sacrifice to the bookkeeper notching
stolen promises into the curtain. The
cloud man humming to himself in the corner.

The Mario Theory

I've only been home three days
and I'm already scared
of resurrection is a cheap
trick. The theory implies
we have multiple lives,
and every time we die
we switch consciousness

to opening the door for
the cat again. I have
varnished it on every
sunny day so the rain
does not pitter patter
the hinge into my

love for you is greater
than it was on universes
one through eight,
and I think we can
recreate the ninth
if you allow me to

bathe in the blood
of course I will be
around to tell you
how to program the
universal remote, but
I don't know if it'll be you,
you, or another you.

Drunk Poem

There's a cornucopia in the iris,
we work the fields and plough
ourselves over the bones of
my wide goes to bed too late
for me to write my day.

Everything reveals itself
eventually, as if muted by magic
and gilded by your hand is
softer than a glove of violence.
I am working through the night.

The kerning is away with the fairies,
we are all learning to be instantly
attracted to force. Whether
sheer or nearby accidental
conceive my child and kill me,

O black widow, O silent
sniper, O heavenly arc-
angel hyphenated and loose.
I am ripe for the ready set
whip and coulter. I am best

read seeded in an early
winter; the sky still blue,
the night settling early, and
the labour manual in luminous
volumes increasing by shadow.

My Little Sign of No Spy

Spring was lifted,
Heart. His tail and
Nose. His warmed
Rays.

As rose, sun morning;
Spring organ music of
Sound, faint pricked
Ears.

Tingle made life
New. Scents green
Of the full fresh
Air.

Sung birds – blossom
And bud, sunlight
Stung first. My little
Red

Of flash tell-tale
Saw a clearing forest
The turned best
Friend.

Ahead lay that day's
Sailing-boat, building-
Den, dipping-pond.
Longsleep.

Charms

Gather me up in an old dishcloth
and gently set me to sea.
I am aware I'm awake when I sail
to a freedom that feels barely free.

Call out my name, darling, please make me swear
I heard secrets within every breath
I feel most brave when I'm saved late at night
as I balance between life and death.

Tie me in knots, lover, wrap me tight
in string, top me off with bow.
I am most weak when I weep when I cry
so silently no-one can know.

Gather me close, tender-sweet warm embrace,
cradle me up, let me rest in your arms,
if I am a bracelet on a thin aging wrist
then you, dear, you are the charms.

LS015:
Pale Mnemonic

Stuart McPherson

Legitimate Snack 015

Title: Pale Mnemonic
Author: Stuart McPherson
Originally printed on:
Paper: Munken Lynx Rough (90gsm)
Cover: Iridescent White Glitter Card (220gsm)
Endpaper: Frida Fuchsia flower
(hand screenprinted on to Nepalese lokta paper)
Titles: Rothwood
Text: Etna

1 run of 40

Upbringing

I associate to remember
what is cut

A knife in a pile of excuses
for knives

Photographs or smoke

We stood beside the
lilac trees

Its butterflies

The cabbage whites
that lived

Are ghostliness

Or the way
I mistook them

For communion

Your spoken words
placed upon my tongue

Dry as wheat

How heavily you
laid across my shoulders

Wooden

As a yoke

Genealogy

Ushering wind into a   pale bag
Knotted   and left to howl

A blueness steeped in a paltry sky
where its limp moon floats

       and left to season

A thin crescent   a razorblade
Shapes of bodies   oozing secrets

    Limbs in the water waiting to be
sewn
         Reportedly, a room without
doors   A crescendo of wailing.
Taxidermy as
                spectator sport

How I Learned to Talk

'For God's Sake' is similarly toned

   As my pen scratching the same
leaning *T* into *To*

Dear Mother, Happy Birthday

   The same way I learned to push
metal through
                To dice vegetables
To teach my daughter how to tie
laces.

If I could pull out my tongue,
I would salt it,
        and send it
           straight back to you

Immovable Observance

His body   all hollowed out and skin,
an acetate thinness
                    Glided past
At least in my lumbered separation
            Beckoned escape from the
cold corners of a   cold day
The carcass of a spider,
           Its siblings in the net
Ignoring play, and the polite need for
attentiveness in the field where we
                  laid out the lambs
This Lent, or the apparent non-ending of it

I followed to the corner
            Climbed inside his legs   *my legs*
Pushed into his arms   *my arms*

In disguise, walked back around
            The disappointment of my steps
                  revealed as an echo
In the roofs of their
quietly
            chewing
                    mouths

Gifted

Forty-three sheets of paper
The first one new   loosely taped
Unfolding like a lank mouth
Nearer the floor with every rip revealing
and rewarded
With a silence l swallow down
Gently rippling from the sacrum
to the cervical spine like a   vertical
                      bleed

Passing the paralysed parcel
The circumference of another year
And between layers   visible indifference
Some *ham-fisted paternity*
A midnight bicycle thrown into a black
canal.   *insurance scams*
The way you extracted life from the
honeybees
Whatever memories linger when I'm alone
They make me think that   somehow
I'm meant to feel more than just laying on
my side   with this hexagonal emptiness

Many happy returns then,   sweet heresy

Blue Anemones

An arc is thrown into air

and held

              momentarily

until its wetness feels the floor

As a snake becoming the sea is
skeletal   then formless

Its blue lakes
           run the
                  gaps

Blisters a ceiling

dying
           to
                  fall

Redecorates with the pale
mnemonic of
               your fear

Markings on the walls similarly
smeared, and floral

Blue Anemones
Explaining pale fingerprints.
Palms frail lifelines

From yours to mine,
               and me

Sundial

Shadow son, dialled in.
A slanted gnomon in
a bright afternoon

Watching the lengthening
light across the five acres
where his father used to till

A blunt harrow designed
to lift the surface of
skin and bone,

and fashioned in the
deepening furrows.
Alone,   as he *shape shifts*

Matryoshka

The entrance   of my heart
             Vena Cava Inferior
             As labelled

In part   fashioned from
             the night he
             left

Twisted open his small death
             pulled out
             placed snugly
             in my chest

My *atrium*   rapping like his
             fingers on the
             dining room table

To/Dear (...)

When you die,

      I will illuminate
with the ovality

           of a paper lantern

The empennage of a
        distant plane

          Untethered

from the ankle
           of a crow

.

LSO16:
Supercutscene

Rishi Dastidar

Legitimate Snack 016

Title: Supercutscene
Author: Rishi Dastidar
Originally printed on:
Paper: Gmund Cotton Linen Cream (110gsm)
Cover: Tintoretto Ginepro (250gsm)
Endpaper: Pressed floral Leamon (100gsm)
Titles: Titular (Heavy Italic, 14pt)
Text: Himalaya (Regular, 14pt)

1 run of 50

Supercutscene

Kinda kooky right? But it sounds like fun.
She was late, as it was her character note.

So you've clapped your hands and stopped time.

He was to take the train. A gift was to be delivered.

A working knowledge of Catholic theology will also be useful.

'I rowed into a giraffe gorilla.'

What made it all worthwhile was the way she shaped the plaster
in her hands.

but who should blow past me but Methuselah.

He offered his teeth, his fingers, as methods to distract her again.

The lenses were the size of dinner plates.

A flicker of life.

The moral was clear. He just wasn't sure whom it was directed to.

You do not see the carrots shiver with relief.

I've wanted to do it since I was a cub.

Years later, people still wonder how the hurricane started.

Of feeling like a needle that's waiting for its thread.

A sneeze. A bang. A smouldering.

They floated above the pavement: high enough to thrill; low enough to avoid dishonour.

And she sighed again.

Whether I'm frayed by the work I after to do. Whether I'm torn by the load I carry.

'I am asserting the primacy of the hunter over his victuals,' he told the interviewer before addressing the barbell.

He saw the gold against the red and white of his vest.

But still, the door handles gave women something else to fondle.

Intrigued, and looking for an untraditional way to freshen up her wardrobe, she bought two.

If I'd known she was into sweatband S&M, I might have said no to her.

Do not be surprised if you see the three heads of three boars sipping glasses of Malmsey.

I mean, you don't think that the mere presence of blood is enough to constitute being alive.

It said, 'I heart tentacles'.

The message said, 'DON'T WORRY. I'M GOOD AT BEING SNEAKY. X'

Some policemen swore later that the Stasi had trained ideo-logically committed kitties to infiltrate West Berlin.

The couple exchanged glances, then moved closer, so that they could peer in.

The ashes settled into the silent, soft gloop.

You are not leapfrog technology, they say to me.

If your sleep consisted of beating your arms against an aquamarine, blankly threatening sky; your eyes empty, head permanently bowed, mouth aching, the cord cutting into your gums.

The emissary from Folderol sparkled uselessly, prettily and noiselessly.

'Like everything in life, you have to dig for it. Go.'

I will sing, and that will make you come back.

She still liked being considered, despite the caveat emptors she wore on her hands.

'Congratulations!' beamed God. 'You got the part!

This is troubling, as she'd gone out on a limb on this case.

Having my ankles as hip bones is novel, but I've been assured that I'll be going into the textbooks now.

The blow torch is also lying back on the floor, exhausted.

You note that the river is dieting to a trickle.

'Congratulations diner. That was your last ever rasher of bacon. Ever.'

He wondered why they kept being sent out like this to preach like this. He was a boy with a white face, who walked past me without making a sound.

Big column in the middle, and I can see into all the other rooms.

In his other hand, he brandished blessings of rosemary the size of traffic lights.

If the walls melted, the walls melted.

No other methods he'd tried had jumped him out of it.

'The purpose of the system is what it wishes to be.

'That's it! Time to test your Bezold-Jarisch reflex!'

Some of us have not reappeared since the frosts and snow came.

What I am saying is: get good at roulette. That's the only su thing.

He couldn't run the risk to his aura.

You walk past, full of beans, as the cliché has it, in a pink gingham dress, before vaulting the telephone wires and land ing on Piccadilly Circus, pulling Eros out of the ground and taking him with you.

The trilby's angle meant that I couldn't see his eyes.

6. Flashbacks, of a sort. Or maybe they are flashforwards.

'I'll call you.'

People wanted a saint. They just didn't want one that was better than them.

He had given her some raspberry bubble bath. He had given her infinite time. He had given her a permanent winter.

She exhaled, a gimlet look in her eye.

A man who said he was the reincarnation of Phineas T Barnum had attached a parasail to him.

Audiences don't want chat about time and probability and infinity.

'I steal stories,' he replied. 'Only the best. Ones that move people.'

'Still, it's your only congregation with permanent smiles.'

When she stayed up to hear him practice, coyly standing at the crack of the door, she was amazed at what the blur of his arms could coax out of a box with a hole, badly wrapped in nylon.

And the mirrors leave the room.

I did what all men do when faced with a problem. Retreated to my shed.

You have always imagined a world without weather to be sunny, but this is false because the very fact that there might be sunlight but no clouds is still 'weather', but just the sort you like.

My surgeon tells me that he's got more absent-minded over the years.

What was most pleasing was the way the stitches started to unweave themselves.

He had been told that he would no longer be spotted in a well-lit urban environment.

'Sorry mac. That's just how things go sometimes.'

Sunglasses the size of hub caps.

I stand here and wait for my eyes to fly away, my stomach to spin, my heart to leave this frame.

Once, in the clinic, a woman had whispered, 'OAB, OAB.'

And I saw you, dancing in it.

I know. I'll sack the psychobabbling fucker when I get out.

Whump. The passport went down on to the booth.

Years later he still woke up dreaming of the way she had winked at him.

He liked most to speed his heart up. He would flick the knife downwards to jump-start the fluttering.

Quick quick slow. Weak weak strong.

But then maybe they knew that I had stolen all the luck in the world.

And his chances of moving up had evaporated.

At least the tyres I was imprisoned in were snug.

'I believe I can fly,' he crooned. He had stolen the voice he was from a child.

'I've been reading a lot of Robert Graves,' he said, 'and he's worked out why there's so much disgrace in the world.

The infantry began to raze the spread before them. Their only duty: to be trenchermen.

She could tell you how old he was without rummaging in his flattened pockets.

LS017:

POLYCHROMATICS

Maria Sledmere

LEGITIMATE SNACK 017

TITLE: Polychromatic
AUTHOR: Maria Sledmere
Originally printed on:
PAPER: Gmund Cotton Linen Cream (110gsm)
COVER: Pastel Pink (210gsm)
ENDPAPER: Pink Gold Vellum
TITLES: Gravesend sans (Medium, 8pt)
TEXT: Mokoko (Regular, 8pt)

1 RUN OF 40

Where colour provides the contours, objects are not reduced to things but are constituted by an order consisting of an infinite range of nuances. Colour is single, not as a lifeless thing and a rigid individuality but as a winged creature that flits from one form to the next.

— WALTER BENJAMIN

Cashless, the snow fell in your dream

three million times osculation

of this surface once was grass, soft silhouette

in pink snow. I scoop masses

of this snow

to carry around for hours. How long

are the kisses that fill my jar

is a person

in megadune, pink snow

I carry in the hard old night

with its cyclone of loneliness,

myriad hail, electrical storm

and the city remembered

once subglacial

pinks on ice.

The snow fell

mottles of stereo pink

in headful of mono

was a meteorite

not from this world, underwater

on sun's invisible sister.

I was a dumb narwhal

in demented tapestry, thirtieth century

with spirals of ivory, I saved you.

Colours train us where to look for details

focusing our attention

in a way that predetermines

what "matters"

writes Melody Jue

in *Wild Blue Media*

I read about the octopus

who would make a rug of bright lichen

tentacular in its woven formlessness

I found on a walk about today

on a board called Farm Work

there are soft pink barnacles, wolf

and tortured horsehair, plum

and custard fungus, star-tipped

reindeer lichen, infinity scarf

worn by the octopus, budget-friendly.

We are tipped out of air in a salt currency.

The octopus displays her colours often

with apparent abandon, not to warn predators

or camouflage; rather

to be wedged in kelp palisade, sexuate

where I visit

sometimes, bearing gifts of ceramics

I place among corals

and other bleached feelings

to be received by these barely glimpsed

gelatinous creatures, the dumbo octopus

and the deepest-

dwelling loss, a giant sea spider

or big red jellyfish, the general isopod or

stingray colossus. Who sees us

as we lay to sleep?

You awake to orange in significant quantity

on a checkerboard floor in the year 2030.

Notice the tapestry depicts

a jar at the window, spilling

pink snow from its leaky milieu.
I was stapled to pale blue aquarium walls
and fantasies of former life on land;
I tease at the edible threads.
Perverse among crocuses
to collect back
from originary lock
a fresh, lascivious spring
turn to splash magic—
I fill it with websites.

The gatherings of hay were celadon
out of season. Try explaining "twilight"
at civil dinner party, in some other universe
am I on a webcam, falling asleep
in pale blue crinoline, underwater
in dream of your summer
a fixed-term employment
contract issued to ghosts.

At a place called The Coast
I am serving twilight lattes
of skinny rose snow
skimmed from the sea
to members of the bourgeoisie.
They tip with pockets of lenticular corals.

I take the rug wherever I go.
I have flown in its clouds
shrill as some bright eyes
of lyric ache, say we tried very hard
to make colour therapy.
Today is a classical grey sky.
Today is a very strong idea
of purgatory, pink headphones
in tracksuit reality, yet it snows?
The comic tempo of situationist milks
had leaked on the internet.
I'm doing circuits.
Keep your hand away

from the underside of the rug
backing material
as you work the tool
to avoid cutting yourself.
The milk crystallised pink snow
falling in twilight
collects beneath my yellow lid.

You hold it warm
at the end of world, agreeable
grey kind of weather.

This all on loan.
I want to thank you for lichen
and starlight; hyperlinks
collect in my syntax.
I sit in my blue pyjamas
of fake silk, drawstring
dreams to rain.
The green jar
is overfull with pain.

Morning candied
and pilled, pink goop

of a Flower Moon, orange
from Wolf Moon—
what do I know?
Side effects
include full employment,
lightheadedness, slurring
insomnia of the bees.

Amorphous structures
are cast in my dream
authorities of habitat.

Once I was
a ceramicist's apprentice;
I auditioned for the most expensive silicon
carbide, nitride, zirconium oxide, special foams
and residue of pink snow
a high-quality software, not to be compounded

at the celadon window
of fodder, heavy light.
You can live here
inclined to melt.

The meteors make excuses.
Something changes in you
once sunlight emolliates on our jellyfish skin
like I might type at the future of weather
or die softly
in bunny-eared gardens
where you hand me a carton of lilac
I could drink for good or choose not to.
The whole shimmerology of emotional blues,
pinks, extinct greens and yellows. I tip
my jar to the clouds that night.
I open my satchel for hours.
I am the water of finite proportion
or vitreous levy, run over.
Remember the snow in lieu of cheap stars
you were putting the bins out

colour-blind to all recycled flowers,

blush dumb

lain in spindrift

I, chrysanthemum

of pink snow

to be picked up

or rolled out of air, out of revenue

LS018:
St

Mary Anne Clark

Legitimate Snack 018

Title: St
Author: Mary Anne Clark
Originally printed on:
Paper: Gmund Cotton Linen Cream (110gsm)
Cover: Cosmos Pearl Antique Gold (300gsm)
Endpaper: Gampi Bougainvillea (90gsm)
Titles: Craw Modern (Italic, 12pt)
Text: Essonnes (Text Regular, 8pt)

Number:

1 run of 40

something endureth forever and it'd better be good
if I'm gonna say something then I'd better make it good
do you number yourself among the great and the good?
the saint and the monster are back for good.

St

When I was small and desperate for sainthood
I walked backwards down streets for a year.
Dully inconvenient, but not without peril.
Streets and saints: straits between place and place,
chaining hand to hand, to hand us on to somewhere.
Thinking of the old warriors who contorted
and were contorted for a cause, the old worriers
who couldn't let it go, I couldn't let it.
I linked my antics to God. It's fair to say
that I was coming at things from the wrong angle.
It didn't last because real saints, I think,
like streets, see where they need to go and go there.

Hagiography

I saw Christopher, eye-sore of a man,
giant arm-span, head of a dog,
hefting his harm about. I saw him
all quiver and readiness stand in the river.
Christopher, carry the Christ-child across,
milk-mild held in your hideous jaws.
I wish you could carry my child like that,
like that weight of love was more than the world.

Note: They read him wrong, Christopher, canine for Canaanite.
So foreign it hurts. See certain icons in which he looks up to
howl psalms at the moon, his muzzle made tender in the light.

†

Ursula, the sea-wind sting-lashed her hair
into my face; thin-wristed, abashed-ankled
sea monster with her seething coral of virgins.
She displaced the water, travelling as fast
as the earth, her kiss was a sea urchin.
Schoolgirls running into the wind, you stayed
out too late, you wet your feet
too fully in the spouse-less sea, you knew
too much and too little – now you are sent up,
now you are laid in your small beds.

Note: A burial ground in Cologne: small bones are thought
to be those of the slaughtered virgins, Ursula and her crew.
Controversy grew when some of the relics were found to be the
skulls of mastiffs, pups with furless muzzles coldly nuzzling
the teat of the soil.

Simeon Stylites, high-rise trip-tease,
I saw him, I think, like a mote in the eye,
a beetle on a stem, a giant on a diet:
there are eyes on stalks at Si on his stalk.
His vertebrae walk step-wise to the clouds,
his eyes shut in the silence of air, of prayer:
you have taught us many things of use,
and sluiced us with wisdom from on high,
but come down, come down, your mother, your mother.

Note: Similar stylites sprang up in Simeon's name, a disparate
forest of those mutually alone over our heads.

One walked down a hill towards me,
head in hands – his head, his hands.
They unstopped you Denis, like a bottle,
but you were, for a while, unstoppable, leis-
          urely,
I heard you preach, taking measured steps
and cradling that kind jaw so casually,
almost as if those wine-sweet words
you poured to the lees for us could come
any time, but it might as well be now.

Note: One of the Holy Helpers, Denis, head-less, was patron
of headaches – it's handy to have someone who really
understands.

I saw one who gave the poor
her dowry, as would have been; to the widow,
a word and a floury fist of dough –
a spice-cake and a sharp look to the orphan.
Lucy, lead-weight, dead-weight to the hands –
the men and their taut-necked oxen couldn't pull you
from the place where your sensible shoe was planted,
rooted as deep as the heart; for you
had the art of God's own inconvenience,
the snowfall, the floodplain, the leaves on the line.
Oh pray for me that I be a hindrance;
oh give me the strength to be dully, doltishly,
phlegmatically, blockishly, beautifully immoveable.

Note: When guards came to carry Lucy to a brothel as
punishment for her inconveniently charitable life, she became
by a miracle impossibly heavy.

†

I saw I don't know what and it was
Clare, cropped hair, head like a knucklebone,
girl who had everything chose to have nothing.
Father loses a daughter and next thing
she's all over the town like a map, what a sight,
barefoot and skin drawn tight as a cold snap,
all shoulder-blades and silence crouched in the doorways.
But when you walked out with nothing but the sacrament
to the edge of town, past the last houses
and stood watching I thought you were perfect.
And when the approaching army saw you
they turned back and ran without knowing why.

Note: I've seen the place where Clare lived and died and it's the
quietest place there is.

Paul

I know I know – it's dark here at last
the night-sleeve sweeps over the page of the ground
here, heavy, the air is still –
my heartbeat is tensed for a glorious theft
nothing left behind – my cries, take them –
there's thick fog my friends – I call to you
I send my soul to the twelve-armed road
waiting sinner – still homecoming –
oh zenith of this knowing – not knowing of this zenith oh
homecoming – still-waiting sinner,
to the twelve-armed road I send my soul
to you I call my friends – there's thick fog
behind my cries (take them) – nothing left
for a glorious theft – my heartbeat is tensed –
the air is still here, heavy
the rage of the ground sleeps under the dawn
at last – it's dark here I know, I know.

Peter/Basilisk

I knew you all along my best beheld,
my only one. And everybody knows
that I'm the reason. Slight as love, as strong,
and never right enough not to be wrong.
When the cock crows take me; my skin is candid
as a night-long coal and I am past forgiving.
I look you in the eye and it is finished.
It's finished and – I look you in the eye.
Forgiving, and I am past as a night-long coal.
My skin is candid when the cock crows. Take me:
never wrong enough not to be right,
as strong as love, as slight, and I'm the reason
that everybody knows. My only one,
my best beheld, I knew you all along.

How To Be Good

I saw I don't know what, and it's the moon.
It's almost night and almost home and it's
there, stepping backwards bigger now than ever,
slap bang above the middle of the street.
Like anything's worth trying when the world's
involved. So many people are involved.
I'm considering my approach to love and hate
and how to get all the embracing done
and all the fighting done. I'm worrying
about how little of it all I've done.
But if I ever climb this holy hill
I'll be so glad to see the way the dark
laps at the moon. Like how when I was small
and tried imagining the universe
I could only see
the rough-edged blue black wash,
to which, with a brush, a little more might be
added when I could, a little more.

LS019:
KAYFABE

Colin Bancroft

LEGITIMATE SNACK 019

TITLE: Kayfabe
AUTHOR: Colin Bancroft
Originally printed on:
PAPER: Arena Uncoated Rough (120gsm)
COVER: Dark Blue Lustrulux (250gsm) [SMACKDOWN]
COVER: Lampone Sirio (290gsm) [RAW]
ENDPAPER: DDT Piledriver (90gsm)
TITLES: Allstar (Regular 12pt)
TEXT: Benguiat Pro ITC (Book, 8pt)

1 RUN OF 40
[20 SMACKDOWN blue // 20 RAW red]

How a Guide to winning the Royal Rumble is a Guide for Life

The first thing you need is a good slice of luck as to when you enter. Nothing good ever came from being the first one in. More people have walked on the moon than have won from the number one position, remember that. You have no friends, not here. They will boot you in the face and toss you out like yesterday's trash. Skulking helps as does hiding under the ring. A bag of thumbtacks or a barbed wire bat are not illegal. Never run towards the ropes because someone will send you over them. Likewise never climb too high because there is always someone ready to push you off. If Kane arrives then you have already lost. Always walk down the ramp. Enthusiasm will only get you killed & playing to the crowd is usually a big mistake. Perhaps the best piece of advice I can give you is that if you do go over the top rope, hold on for dear life, fight and claw as you dangle over the precipice, because no one has ever been victorious when both their feet have touched the ground.

CRASHED AND BURNED THROUGH A TABLE AFTER MISSING A SWANTON BOMB OFF THE TOP OF A STEEL CAGE
SURVIVOR SERIES 2001

There's a moment at the end of the match
When Jeff Hardy is on top of the cage
And all he has to do is drop to the floor
And he and Matt would win the titles.
No fireworks or grandstanding in that,
But then Jeff turns and sees D'Von
Prone on the table fifteen feet below,
Just lying there in the middle of the ring.
And all he has to do is drop to the floor
And he and Matt would win the titles.
But Jeff couldn't resist, and you see
The moment when he decides to say fuck it
Cross his face, and he lifts his arms up
In a kind of two-gunned shoulder shrug,
As though it was always going to play out
That way, and he dives off as a thousand
Camera flashes light up the arena.
And I have taken something of that moment
With me through the rest of my life,
When it would have been much easier
To drop down to the floor and win the match.
To fall back on the safe option of nothing,
Rather than risk the flashbulb intensity
Of coming across to your desk that morning
And asking you out, with all the air driven

Out of my chest before you had even said yes,
Feeling more alive than if I had just crashed
And burned through a table after missing
A Swanton Bomb off the top of a steel cage.

FACE TURN

I took the beatings for years, like all good faces:
The kicks in the dinner queue,
Pushed down the stairs on the way to lessons,
My clothes dumped in the shower after PE.
And I did nothing, took my vitamins
And said my prayers. Laughed it off.
Played it down, hoped that my silence
Would make me invisible, but it never did.
At night I would walk home the long way
To avoid the shops where I knew they'd be.
What happened to me that Wednesday morning
In Year Nine, in Maths, I don't know.
I remember him sitting behind me, kicking
My chair. I remember asking him to stop,
Repeatedly asking him to stop,
Until I said that if he did it one more time,
If he wanted the chair so god damn much,
I would gladly give it to him.
That I would *turn that son bitch sideways,*
Shine it up and stick it straight up his candy ass.
So he did.
And I wrapped the blue plastic so hard
Around his head that he fell to the floor, crying,
Selling it like he was Mankind at the '99
Royal Rumble and The Rock was using his head
For batting practice.
I got an afternoon detention for that,
And the biggest crowd pop
When I walked in my form room the next day,

Having done what everyone had wanted to do
For years. Not that I condone violence of course,
But he never kicked my chair again.

ENTRANCE MUSIC

Throughout my life I have had entrance music
Running in my head. When I was younger
It was the monotonous refrain of a bass guitar,
Something that any generic jobber would have
As he made his way out to the ring
Before getting his ass whipped by the champ.
Then after I left school and got that job
In the office I would hear The Rock's music hit
IF YA SMELLLLLLL WHAT THE ROCK IS COOKIN'
Every time I thought about what it would be like
To put my manager through a table.
In my twenties, when I got stabbed, I heard the
shattering glass of Stone Cold Steve Austin
As I chased the guy down the street,
Ready to open up a can of whoop ass
Before blood loss made me tag out.
And you better come to my funeral,
Because, I shit you not, the lights will go out
And the lightning will strike and the Undertaker's
Dong will echo through the crematorium
And I will sit bolt upright in my coffin,
Just to see the looks on your faces
As you stare into the eyes of a dead man.

KAYFABE
FOR BEN

All we had in those early years were the kayfabe
Dreams that someday we would make it.
Those nights that we stayed up watching
PPV's, Playing Smackdown! on the Playstation,
Our created characters always looking
Like they had a day-job in a sex dungeon,
And planning our move to Boston to train
At Killer Kowalski's wrestling school.
I mean if Crash Holly can make it.
I still have the Lonely Planet guide that I bought
From Waterstones god knows how many years
Ago, that first small step in our going.
Hundreds of hours spent in the gym together
bulking up. Working those shitty jobs
At Gala Bingo and Weatherspoons
In the hope that one day we would be able
To save enough money just to fuck off and
leave All this behind. We knew deep down
That it was all just a pipe dream, a fantasy
That would never play out in real life
The way that it did in our heads.
But it also saved us in a way, kept us straight,
Pushed us to be the first in our family
To go to Uni, to get off the estate.
And though now we both have jobs we hate
And bills and families of our own,
I still think that tomorrow I might go,
Pack my bag and leave, find somewhere to
train And, without asking you,

OUT OF NOWHERE

If someone were to ask me to describe beauty I would tell them about that Saturday afternoon in the Trafford Centre when we were in Marks and Spensers and you hit that RKO out of nowhere on the mannequin at the front of the store. How you got so much height on your vertical leap, the way your back curved like a ballet dancer as you seemed to tenderly unfurl your arm around its neck, like a lover, before cupping it in your bicep and driving its face down, hard, onto tiled white floor. How the security guard, who looked a little too much like X-Pac, chased you through the lingerie section before you escaped backstage through the fire escape and how I am sure I heard J.R on the tannoy screaming 'By God he is broken in half' as the mannequin's head rolled off towards the baby clothes, looking up at me longingly as though I were Al Snow.

LS020:

One Last Spin around The Sun

Eva Griffin

Legitimate Snack 020

Title: One Last Spin Around the Sun
Author: Eva Griffin
Originally printed on:
Paper: Arena Uncoated Rough (120gsm)
Cover: Intensive Orange (210gsm)
Endpaper: Sun & Floral Moon Vellum (90gsm)
Titles: Antarctican Headline (Book, 14pt)
Text: Politica (Regular, 9pt)

1 run of 40

On the first day of the end she finds old nails
under the couch

hugging skirting boards,
in seldom open drawers.
Each one fills a teacup at her bedside
and dreams of coffins closed tight
by her hands; the hammer
a constant sound, a comfort.

She believes that AI will save her

At night, she sees her brain scooped
into leftover ice cream tubs
and in the morning

opening the freezer
her brain is gone,
the ice cream eaten. Only unbreakable

bags of frozen peas and sweetcorn remain.

Interlude I (on the desire to be eaten)

Consider our bodies fine, young machines
and the plugging of one to another
is the only means of achieving that
fingers-into-fists feeling like,
you ball up your hand and put it –
the whole, entire thing –
into your mouth while he watches.
It emerges wet
covered in yourself.
You are the spit,
that sheen. Oil-slicked like Italian bread.
Dip yourself lower. No, I said, *lower*.

She slices a clementine with a hand saw

the juice running out is so real
          the kitchen is now a fruit bowl

and she a pip in the orange stream
          she sucks on pulp in a distracted way
and Netflix asks

if she's still there
          she nods

her lips sour-swollen
          rough-rind fingers drying
sticky-delicious

a single seed falls into her lap
          she hopes it takes root

She performs a live reading of her insides

talking to strangers she met
in the bathroom of a sparked-up club.

She shows a glowing cut fingertip to
bleary-eyed girls who keep

crying out names
she doesn't recognise:

M—! M—! L—! J—!
The consonants spit down their chins.

One of them is puking in a stall,
her toilet-papered black stilettos

sticking out needle-dark on the tiles.
She is tempted to pray like a sugar-drunk girl.

Bending her blue-bitten legs to 90 degrees,
to something that feels comfortable, she

begins purging all the synonyms for love.

Interlude **II** (on the merits of death)

the empty plastic bottles are branded drinks
she knows by heart and feels now
fizzing her arteries
setting her blood alight
swan necks stretch to beak the cans
the liquid leftovers of people together
she imagines the swans taking to the bank
feathers puffed pretty for the boys
they drink deep let the bubbles come
flat-footed skimming the water
they sing old folk songs to the fishes
bills breaking into a smile
at their long last useful names
but back here the swans are silent
she rubs a pebble between thumb and forefinger
considers throwing herself

She receives a message

Swallow first the blue.
Throw yourself on the floor.
Roll like thunder on linoleum.
Nothing sadder than an ending,
but welcome all the same.
Let the bright light of the kitchen
settle on your tongue
like a sunrise,
and when you spit at men they will cry
silent faced with spring.
Other people fear the tenderness of skin
but not us (yes, you, and me, also).
In church we eat the body of God,
a miracle how it fits so well
in the roof of your mouth.
Blood looks like it would taste sweet.
Why not drink up?
Did you hear me?
I said, *drink up!*
Without water, the pill will linger
in your esophagus, spark slowburn.
It will feel like dying.

She takes to dying like a vibrating cat

on paws watching a hamster wheel turn.
The world still looks the same spinning
out of control like that,
fast on your feet like that.

She pins a silver moth to the cork
board above her desk
and watches it fight
beat-beat against the backing.

Little wings making little sounds;
not the thundering end but
the softest evaporation,
the gentle wet of the glass.

Couldn't you just die like that?
Curled up on the couch watching
a small animal run,
watching a winged thing fail to fly;
wouldn't it be so peaceful?

She makes origami butterflies

bottle-nosed in the back of a pub
napkins are never not stained
the smell of now gone fingers
that once cupped dozens of peanuts

the impression of those salt-burned lips
pressed then to a pint glass and guzzling
each one with an orange segment

we are all collecting half-moons
in pursuit of wholeness
not realising the full-fistedness of an asteroid!

that ending brands a mark bigger than you
rough-knee'd at the altar spitting
seeds from your last last drink

she gathers her ornamental wings
blows a stale song into the bottle
wipes her mouth clean
leaves

Acknowledgements

001: Aaron Kent

002: Dominic Leonard

003: Sarah Fletcher

004: J H Prynne

005: Suna Afshan

006: Wayne Holloway-Smith

006.1: Margot Holloway-Smith & Wayne Holloway-Smith

007: Imogen Cassels

008: Richard O'Brien

009a: Naush Sabah

009b: Naush Sabah

010: Kyle Lovell

011: Dom Hale

012: Jenna Clake

013: Astra Papachristodoulou

014: Aaron Kent

015: Stuart McPherson

016: Rishi Dastidar

017: Maria Sledmere

018: Mary Anne Clark

019: Colin Bancroft

020: Eva Griffin

LAY OUT YOUR LEGIT UNRESI